Gallery Books
Editor Peter Fallon

JUNIPER STREET

Vona Groarke

JUNIPER STREET

Gallery Books

Juniper Street
is first published
simultaneously in paperback
and in a clothbound edition
on 25 March 2006.

The Gallery Press
Loughcrew
Oldcastle
County Meath
Ireland

ISBN 1 85235 398 8 *paperback*
    1 85235 399 6 *clothbound*

A CIP catalogue record for this book
is available from the British Library.

Contents

JUNIPER STREET

Ghosts

Not exactly. Something like breath on your cheek
or an aftertaste of summer, years ago; one,
two metallic notes with the cadence of a name;
silverfish throwing your reflection off a beat.
Or a peony petal blown onto your path.

I don't think so. The children know.
They breathe ghosts into January
that stand for the split second it takes
to take us in, and then they're off
as though released, like figments of the air.

Windmill Hymns

In the shadow of the windmill we put down our lives.
Something about its girth and ballast, the sun on its back,
its shiftless, amber absolute foreclosed on other options.
We put down our lives as if for a moment — a break for tea
or to deal with an enquiry in the yard — and something about

its dereliction shut down at once on the chance of things
ever picking up again. Now, seven years on, this is us
finding the storeys equal to our time and too ornamental.
Even its decay does not refuse the compliment of sunshine,
the way the moon rubs up against it, or clouds distract

themselves upon its brim. What we were after was a stopgap
for the lives we thought we'd live, that wouldn't be banked
in small talk, disappointments, lack of cash; the intended,
blue-sky lives that would have us tilting at an evening do,
with arms like French film stars and mouthfuls of moonlight

to slip us downstream into bed. That was then. I lie. It never was.
This instead is the relief of getting nowhere, of knowing
from the start how it must end. The same momentum,
selfsame pace that drags itself and all its consequence
over the bones of another rattled year. I suppose, at some point,

it will stop, and all the shunt and grind of the day-to-day
come creaking towards another new conclusion, a new plan:
the last sacks loaded, the carts dismissed, handshakes,
gates pulled shut from the outside and then a silence
gaining on the sails, settling there, the way birds do, the air,

the damp, the mould will all do now. How long before the wood
lets itself down on willowherb that finds itself at bay in shuttered light;
before the doors give up the ghost; the floors shrug the way windows
cannot bring themselves to do, until local lads with slingshots
and deadeyes see to them? How long until the weeds take hold

and starlings, like quicksilver, like silverfish, like a fastness
of silver spilled out on the stones? And us? We don't move.
Our way of holding on, of saying, 'We've stayed too long',
is like the way the children have of stopping play
to stand stock-still under the whir of starlings' hide-and-seek.

That what's missing should be called 'the coping' makes me
want to lay my face against the stone; let ivy root in my teeth;
weather grout my skin, my eyes take on the evening and its down.
Let my children stand within an inch of my life, so the way
their breath aspires could be the sky, or something close, to me.

The Couch

A gap-minder on the Gortmore road
when the cattle are on the move,
I am flap and holler, borrowed bluff,
and none of it will last long enough
to see a ruck of them scatter,
the brown of them take any hold.

Wait on a while, say thirty years,
for one to stray through the gate
of my sitting room, to come to a standstill
by the hedge of the window sill, to squat
and haunch, to lie low as a brown heat
splayed for refuge in the gap of four a.m.

To Smithereens

You'll need a tiller's hand to steer this through
the backward drift that brings you to, as always,
one fine day. August 1979. A sunlit Spiddal beach.

Children ruffle the shoreline. Their nets are full
of a marvellous haul of foam and iridescent sand
and water that laughs at them as it wriggles free.

They hardly care: they are busy spilling buckets
of gold all over the afternoon. But further back,
something spreads over the beach like scarlet dye

on the white-hot voice of the radio. The mams
and aunts pinned onto Foxford rugs put down
their scandalous magazines and vast, plaid flasks

as a swell from over the rocks showers them
with words like *rowboat, fishing, smithereens.*
You hear it too, the news that falls in slanted beats

like metal shavings sprayed from a single,
incandescent point to dispel themselves
as the future tense of what they fall upon.

Let's say you are lifted clear of the high-tide line
into another order of silence. Exchange the year.
The cinema's almost empty. She has taken you

to *Gandhi* at the Ritz. You are only a modernist
western wall away from the Shannon and the slipknot
of darkness the river ties and unties in the scenes.

Her breath is caught up in it: she's nodding off.
Her head falls back on the crimson plush and then
her carriage bears her on and on, shunting towards

the very point where all the journeys terminate
with the slump and flutter of an outboard engine
reddening the water with its freight. It's here

that every single thing casts off, or is brightly cast,
into a flyblown, speckled plural that scatters tracks
in the heat and dust of the locked projection room.

The railway bridge one up from ours shakes out
each of its iron rails in readiness, and she is woken
by words that spill over the confluence of the Ganges

and the Shannon at our backs. 'To smithereens?',
she says. 'I'm pretty sure it's Indian. It means
to open (like an Albertine); to flower.'

The Undercurrent

Anywhere. So long as there's a flicker of sea,
a far-fetched train, a lighthouse nodding off
between tea-time and that moment when
your father brightly takes you by the hand
to a place that is the opposite of home.
'Not over the rocks in darkness, Paddy.
You don't mean to tell me that.'

The Local Accent

This river is pronounced by granite drag.
It is a matter of inflection, of knowing what
to emphasize, and what to let drift away,
just as a slipping aspen leaf makes barely a flicker,
one gaffe in the conversation between the current
and the flow; a stifled yawn, a darkness reimbursed;

while, underneath, the thing that falls through shadow
is full of its own occasion. Weighty and dull,
it longs for water, the lacquer and slip of it,
the way it won't allow for brightness on its back,
but flips around to where its fall is a wet-wool,
sodden thing about to break at any moment, and undo.

Something is coming loose like aspen leaves, or froth.
Or maunder, letting itself down like rain into a river
immersed in getting on with what it separates:
the sulk of damp soil; the stiff articulation of the shore,
the giddy vowels sprayed over the drag and ebb
of voices leaking through the rain over the town.

Everything arrives at a standstill under the bridge.
The town grips the river and all the words for elsewhere
or for being there have had their edges worn off
and their meanings powdered to a consonantal darkness
where they dissolve, like happenings, into traffic
and asphalt, or otherwise, in the river and its silt.

This river is pitched so far from the sea
it announces itself in elision, as though everything
unsaid could still bed down in depth and unison,
underwriting words for going on and every other way
in and out of this one place. Excepting the blood-red
trickle of sky, and what it overrides, what slips beneath.

Athlones

A town racked on a river, too far in,
too cosseted by land to be tossed
and turned by anything so flighty as a sea.

Always under the governess eye of Lough Ree,
bearing down in mourning silks
with a sudden tetchiness on boats

that splutter their poorly learned past tenses
much too late. The same boats on the river
are like firstborns in a county family

propped up on surnames and wide berths
on a current lately civilized, its face
scrubbed clean and all its trawl

of Latin verbs and parlour songs
boxed clean away for tomorrow morning's
class. This is a river taken in hand

and made to march along the fastness
of the Castle and the Barracks wall: it keeps
the swell of Connaught well at bay.

A two-faced river, holding the line between
the Pale and Irishtown, the to-and-fro of siege
or confiscation, dual strategies of granite and edict.

A river kept in check, though dampness
slakes the rights and wrongs, the black
and white of its unequal board

where all the lines cast themselves off
to be submerged in what cannot keep quiet,
or in tow. All its words have been vouchsafed

in the low-slung building opposite the church
that put its toe in the water once and froze,
eye to eye with upper decks and punters

waving in at readers picking past the watermark
for a change of plot or a first edition
of the way things ought to be.

Its marbled covers might anticipate a sunlight
that could open out a river's darknesses
as onyx slips or deckled, gold-leaf pages.

The apartment windows jostle for its preference
like dancers primmed in shoes too small,
their candied *thank yous* quite sucked dry

and their bouquet of responses clasped too close.
Such light as ventures in their recess
advances in shifts of obligation and poor grace,

stammers a thin compliment and is lured away
by a river just then letting fall a beaded string
of laughter on a wildly polished floor.

The same light tinkles down through Northgate Street
like someone running late, all streaming hair
and necklaces that chink like moorings

in a breeze, only to trip on the butcher's awnings
or be splayed in Burgess' window like a pomegranate
on an oilcloth, spilling out some exotic largesse.

It roots then in the florist's bins for cellophane
to dabble in, for colour to be sweet-talked
into giving its metallic sheath the slip.

The child with the stick of rock knows how it goes:
he is holding up the wrapper so it crinkles into rainbows
on his palm. In the Genoa Café, the girl manoeuvring

her Coke like a hand-mirror to snare the arc of brilliance
on the cloth knows too. So does the man angling a suitcase
to entice a thread of it from the swags of a plastic raincoat

coming through. A car goes past him once,
its fender spilling a hoard of light on the asphalt
and his shoe. Or the wrist that is opening a window

on the second floor clips the sun with the face of a watch,
and sprays shavings of it down on the highlights of a head
just then emerging from Estelle's Salon. Or the woman

with her bag of books turning her head to check for cars
so her glasses flick a shimmer from the river
over the bulkhead shadow of St Peter's and St Paul's.

Or the sparkler on another woman's hand
slewing announcements all over town, with
a rumour of charm in every unmatched word.

Like the saffron accent of awnings
on Indian stalls in Market Square
leaning into a clatter of hangers

that fills the seams of dresses that were
too much even when the Ritz stood still,
décolleté and shoulder-hunched,

with a hemline skirting the river
like a cotton thread spun out
between Calcutta and Hollywood;

between a full-frontal prairie sunset
and a midland dawn; between two
provinces and two elective ends.

The Galway train declaims
the middle ground, cleaves the river
to an agitated squall, and takes

hardly more than a minute to cross
the bridge, shake out its wingtip
carriages and take off again

to another place that is a fraction closer
to something about to happen
or to conclude a sweet arrangement with

a reason to go on or to go under
at the point where more than accent
slips between *at one* and *alone*,

washing up against the urge to be,
at last, *at home*, pacing over paths
that cast off as I do, in a bed of words,

loose as years ago, and coursing still.
That could, at any second, come
asunder in a darkening hour, or gather

as pleats of rain into a pleated river.
What matter? Its end will still engage
with gold and promises, and nothing

about the gunmetal sheen of the pavement
or the flurry of people with one purpose
in their minds can alter that. So let blinds

be drawn, cars spill muck and piecemeal darkness
on his shoes. Let the woman step out of Estelle's,
uncurl her umbrella, then head off; let the flowers

contract, the pomegranate wither,
the conversation in the Genoa pick up
in the half-light of confidences almost spilled,

a gleam of observations over tea. Let readers
borrow their new order of words: stood in the door
of Fr Mathew Hall, they are sentries waiting

for the castle to brighten, for the church to lift
its veil of winter, for their cars to be no longer
lost to them in the swell of Market Square.

Let jackdaws overawe the bastion,
gulls pierce the Shannon's tireless drone,
traffic pick up from the lights and carry on.

Let computers wind down, office doors
conduct their two-step to the tune of what falls
between *See you tomorrow* and *Oh, by the way* . . .

Step out a while. Those footfalls could be stitches
in an overcoated dusk. The river soars alongside;
evening attends. The wind chimes in the Gallery

set aside their rufflings for the night. The final note
of their cadenza could be the first in the waltz
that plays over and over in the Royal Hotel

as the calendar clicks into place and all the clocks
keep time. The sound of them is like smithereens
of coloured glass; a smattering of rain on the ash trees

of Accommodation Road; like the tinkle of light
on a river learned by rote, if not by heart. The sky
concedes. Any minute now will come release.

Song

for Conor

Between the skiffle
of rats in the attic
and the *aon-dó-trí*
of my heartbeat

and the rest
is something
I can't fathom.

A car rumbles
over Auburn.
A stray lets fly.

And though
it will be years
before we meet

I know now
who stirs
that blackbird
into song.

The Return

The bricked-up door still comes as a surprise
though the new roof struts, like a punchline
to an old one about a slack gable and rain.
I know this house: I wrote our summer here
into words that closed over years ago, and still
I'm back to pick over the same grass as though
I've just come up from the lake with my hair all wet
and you are waiting for me on the porch.
Even your hand stops as I unhook the gate
and there it is, our young day, like the blue of your eyes,
a noticed, simple thing that leaves me dumbfounded
in a half-hearted ruin. My hand on the door admits me
to those months where our lives bedded down in layers
I could no more uncouple now than your wrist
could turn some key or other and have us both
walk out beyond this final door, into the glare
of our release, another headlong day.

The Stain

A spray of waiters flecks the afternoon
just as you appear behind the glass, quizzical, alone,
as though nothing could keep you further off,
not the drifting window nor the table turning
on a sixpence of regret; not the glint of silver
lighting on whatever it is we're likely to do next.

I could have done with seeing how you coped.
Instead, there was your mouth outlining the stain
my plate offered the cloth; your hands printing
the one wine glass with telltale promises.
So what of the linen and its complete sweep:
what are we to do with so much hope?

Slow Set

The music from the house party over the way
bristles a scrag of lawn and at least two rows of roofs.
It slips through my open window, bracelets creaking,
out of breath, like a spiky teenager with things to say
(bulletins from a border region, translations from a dialect)
she's full sure the likes of me won't understand.

Imagine, at forty, falling in love with my perfected youth
or the version of it that gathers twenty of us
into a squat, inhaling each other's rampant breath
with some big-breasted, cupolar song. We close our eyes.
We wish our full lives to be so lush and abject,
the way the climactic guitar solo and its exhaled echo are.

It might as well be the orange scent of bougainvillea
in a basement flat. It comes so wistfully and so blatantly
unsure of why it does, like the most beautiful boy
in the room who is walking towards you even now
with your name just about to dive from his tongue
into the sky-blue lagoon of your hands settling on his waist.

Imagine. I lived then like an unworn watch
gaining by the new time on what it has outgrown,
the Dubonnet we drank in ersatz accents,
the eyeliner that lent us gravitas, Ultravox,
Ozymandias, lurex, hair gel, Blake, hitch-hiking
on a wayward road only to find ourselves pursued

by Shelley's *car of light* in deeper shades of mascara
that baubled like DNA on threads that finally strung out
all my storylines, the parting in my daughter's hair,
my son's clean spine, the longer gap between things happening,
the way his breath advances and retreats, the whole shebang,
the Clash box set, Joy Division, Tichborne's *froste of cares.*

Over the way, the party has spilled out into the yard.
Someone shouts, 'Another lie'. I'd say he's alone already
and she's back inside, dancing in the dark-eyed boy
she picked out on the bus. But I don't exist. My eyes rehearse
a consummate invisibility. The music hardens. I give up,
forget myself, believe they don't play slow sets anymore.

We Had Words

Another hurricane, the third this month, strikes at the heart
of a city far from here. Tomorrow, its leftovers will fill our drain
and leak into the basement to advance on our low-tide mark
a seepage shot with grit and aftermath. My sleep tonight
will be a skimming stone affair: every hour fulfilling an ellipsis
predicted by the last. This day, all day, is hypothetical.
When it steals inside an offhand dusk, not even I
will muster a send-off beyond the thought of dust in darkness,
a breathless stowaway, like your words on the flip side
of my tongue, one almost completely slipped inside another.
I was saying, likening the way you like to single out
a single word to bear the weight of this, to boarded windows
and spineless pines bent double in thin air; cars afloat
on streets that have lost the run of themselves by now;
a casket in a clutch of branches, an item of clothing
tied to a TV aerial, for help. It bypasses us completely.
Your full leg, white as that whiplashed shirt, has drifted
over mine. A siren flares on the pike. It plays itself out
in hours perched on high ground; our breath brimming over;
our new words islanded and arch, to steer us wide of harm.

Call Waiting

Three times I call, three times you're engaged.
You know I am incoming, according to the voice:
my call heralds itself with two round pips,
beads on a chain of intimate, dead air
coiled like the flex around your index finger now
as you stand in the kitchen of the house where I am not
and where, upstairs, is the ring he gave her,
that she gave to me and his dovetailed dress-jacket
she begged me not to wear but I did anyway,
sixteen, blue-haired, all my plans laid out as parallels
marked with a ruler and measured for space
claimed as gracelessly as those black squares
we inked on our fingernails. I must have been nine
when I learned to split a circle three-ways
from just above the centre out, like the Pye sign
in the country town we drove through yesterday.
The boy who told my fortune in Greece
said I had too many lines: they threw him
every which way and he couldn't tell my heart
from head or how the life would span,
but he was right about the indoor garden
I planted with ivy and the little gate that opens
on nothing but its own three arduous notes.
There's a leaf of copper beech in my hand now
and the voice is telling me to hold for a connection.
I tear along the veins and find I am left
with one trefoil that splays like any fish spine
or the crow's feet that have settled round my eyes.
My call is brushing up against yours now
like a ten-cent coin between two fifties in my pocket
or a marble with three colours curled
to skim the arc of two others in its path.
Or like the way your breath on the back of my hand
had three things to say, and none of them got said.

The Boat

It's not what I'd have chosen at this time,
not with the bird's nest scattered on the grate
or the wounded music of the house alarm
coming in waves across darkness and two streets.
This morning the grass at the sycamore was scorched
and these pages were out of sequence on the desk.
What will it be tonight: a small boat lightly edging home
to be met by faces in half-light at the port?
I will know it as the one I have arranged
and must soften with quilts and coats,
make sure you have food to last and an address.
I will push the boat to sea when the oarsman nods.
Wait for me. I have only this to finish.

'I just saw a man with a hole in his head'

My daughter's first sight of a Hindu *Tilak*
strikes me when the girl at the skating rink
turns out to have, not a port wine slick,
but a red admiral, face-painted on her cheek.

The Game of Tennis in Irish History

Blame Lady Alice Howard and her diary of 1873
patrolling the white line around the one green space
at Shelton Abbey where the Parnells, Charlie and Fanny,

banter in and back, skirting the net, filling the hours
between politics and tea. She looks up: a weak breeze riffles
the pages on which she has pinned the afternoon

in Indian ink, and their laughter scatters in choked aspen trees
where sunlight, regardless, upends both the game
and the ambitions of those plainly put-down words.

Another volume: Spring 1921. The diary laments
they have had a blow: a permit for the motor was refused.
Not so in Ballyturin House, where the tennis party

has broken up in salvered tea and calls for a reprise.
Which might itself have been an entry from the diary,
save for the culminating flourish of bodies, one slumped

over the bonnet like an umpire checking the chalk for dust
or the volley of shots like a flurry of late calls, or the opening
account of play stalled on the lodge gates oddly closed.

After that, it's a holding game, put down to delivery,
service skills, to foot faults or to where advantage falls
and to how often the metaphor is required to work the line

between incident and outrage, between the ins and outs
of the intent or outcome, to the calling out or not in
or only just, to the over and eventual out, out, out.

Footnotes

[1] According to Gilbert (1998), this shrew-like quality was not related to size. (p.6)

[2] In 'Spoils', a poem in similar vein, she calls this 'Alabaster'.

[3] 'It rained. The tennis party was abandoned. Charles upset the peonies.'

[4] The logbook records the train arriving closer to 19.08.

[5] from the Irish, meaning 'to exact'.

Parnell

On the mailboat carriage from the Royal Marine,
stones skeet against the window until it breaks.
He sieves a handful of glass from glove to glove
so the shuffle is like money changing hands;
in its shift, he hears syllables silting up
like his name halved on the Irish sea:
one part thinking it will climb on stilts,
the other like the one who waits too long
to be so narrowly, so tacitly turned back.

The British Museum Gift Shop

Concentrated raids. A frenzy of coins to discharge
on some proof of the jaunt has a cluster of schoolkids —
    released from the guided tour —
descend on Ancient Egypt with their brandished cash
and rough-hewn calculations. For a moment,
they are lost in a sally of fruit-drop scarabs,
    hieroglyphic toilet roll, mummy joke books,

pencil-case Pharaohs and the kitty-litter Sphinx.
They lay siege to the counter and the man at the till
    is sorely pressed to hold off their barrage.
Their teacher summons. They fall in line,
mustering in a double row of uniforms and scuff:
their backpacks crammed with treasures (paid for);
    their pockets with hand-picked booty (not).

Archaeology

Call it proof, then, this thing that will survive
like an axehead or the map of a town
where no one ever lived. A story told
as if through frosted glass, all taken up with plot
and happenstance, with the singular moment
of when such-and-such occurred. As if.

Let's look at the detail. Take that woman
stubbing out a cigarette over there. She could be
distressed or paranoid or bored. She says nothing:
she's no help at all. There is only the butt in the ashtray,
the used-up time, the way her coat is slumped
and how she doesn't wear it when she leaves.

Take Jane. She said, 'I lost my key, but anyway
I hadn't locked the door.' Jane knows a thing or two
about moving this along. More than the key,
more than any lock. More than the fragments
of a glazed milk jug can tell about why she threw it
at his upright head, and why he didn't duck.

The stain on the carpet could be spilled milk
or leaking pipe. Patches underneath a wooden seat
might look like prints, but whose — the pregnant woman's
or the nervous man's? And what of all this anyway,
whose evidence grows paler by the hour? What if
only *cigarette* survives, or *leaking pipe*? Or even Jane?

Who then will read a single word or two
and take from this that once there was
a language and a page, a person writing
and re-writing this for days? A hand,
a desk, some form of light, a life inferred
from one of these details. Or maybe all.

Let's skew it with a spray of last night's dreams:
rain that tasted of copper; houses made of silverfoil;
a piglet in a babygro, for fun. And then, at last,
to tie the whole thing up, a woman on an unknown road,
waving a cloth so red it bleeds out on her hand,
the empty road, an inscrutable sky.

The Round House

The hump and clatter of an older sister's sex,
the father putting out to sea in a burlap sleep;
the heft of pelt that is ridden with lice and a spoor
of excrement or semen or caked blood;
the wheeze of that most distant cousin,
the slump of one persistent grandmother;
the general accretion of foul breath:

post holes for the home that draws itself
from the inside out and round again, from the hub
of the hearth to radial sleepers under their communal skins,

out over the heads of the banded oaks reeling in
the dog-legged flight of geese that knows its way
by the grain of the wood in the centre post

where the circle kinks when the child turns over
once in his sleep so his arm slumps
on his mother's side, as though to clasp
or to sweep up these relatively parabolic lines
and to brush them clean away into the corners
that come later on with their allowances, reprieves,
and their straightforward (if too pointed) pecking order.

Chinese Lacquer

Was it you who left the mandarins here
on a table laced with mynah birds
and lotus blossom and, behind them,
the kind of night I could scoop
with an open hand and set down
on a lake so full of itself
it tucks a hem of shadow
into layer on layer of an obvious gloss
and its opacity?

I think I see the mark of your hand
in how the scald of orange upbraids
its pitch and how the sun rebuts it,
hones it to a pointed gold that rims,
like a misplaced ducat,
this oh-so-ravenous depth.

Not even your mandarins perplex it,
nor the fuss of those cankerous, dim birds
or, least of all, that lotus blossom kindling
the warning it had so usefully rehearsed.

It too forgets itself: it gives nothing away.

Quoits

Lost in the forest that hoards its name
is the timepiece that looks to the Clock Museum
to allow for the tick of a river in flood
the name of the house that crumbled to sod
the tock of the watchman's passing car
ashen songs of an old campfire
the cadenza of a silver birch
flagrant light in a seam of quartz
an exact meaning for 'pirogue' or 'quoit'
rain that dispels an ambiguous quiet
the puppet that learned his usage by heart
and flirted, once, with the secondary art
of tying up the loose ends of a voice
that threw itself and came back twice
once as the minute hand, once as the hour
closing in on the heat of the fire
that cracked the glass of the wristwatch
that had kept time with all the clocks
that ever struck beyond a whim
or pointed a wayfarer home
between the straight lines of a dusk
that at his bidding coalesce
into the chinks of a woodpile
where something more than darkness prowls
a late blue slack between its eyes
shadowing his passing trees.

Terms and Conditions

Yet the burnt poet loves the fire.
        — Louis MacNeice

Back into a familiar room, see what you know,
as though you yourself had pulled the thing together
with the drawstring certainty of anything you ever turned
your hand to. But not here, where this room is busy
being someplace else. The pattern on the sofa's wearing thin.
The rug also is withering and even the view is slinking off

to brighter sights elsewhere. Put down your hand
as though from an instrument when the music gives itself up.
What is there? Perhaps a book, an opened envelope, or a box
of safety matches on the desk. You choose. Someone has set
a fire although the window is open so the book becomes
a commentary on what's happening to the room.

You know it. All the words inside are inscribed
on your memory, the way your imprint is upon this place.
The air is stranded when you so much as lift your hand
and every incremental word that marks a place out for itself
is discernible, if you could only see it or look inside.
But your line of vision sags against the window

and you hear again the voice that says, 'All this could be yours'.
It echoes like a debt collector's bell, making even the pink roses
hold their breath, and you're not moving now. Not a whisper.
The book recalls its weight. The envelope addresses itself
again to someone else. The fire is set to warm to another hand.
Even the roses are borrowed from someone else's room.

Bournemouth

Jane of the vanilla skin and me
in the linen room of the Cumberland Hotel
just killing time. She cut my hair.
Or maybe I cut hers. Something, anyway.
We'd pink uniforms, short nails,
jokes about used condoms.
She sang Blondie songs like they were news,
wore blue eyeliner and did extra rooms.
We took a trip to Bournemouth
and ate ice cream with our sandals kicked to shore.
She said, 'Nobody talks of leaving any more.'
Then it was August. We both went home.

Northeast of Nowhere

We're all the same here:
new adventurers, wary,
mortgaged to the hilt;
gardens abloom with
styrofoam and ply.

                    The road's not tarred
                    and the dust gets everywhere.

A white minivan's been seen
circling the estate. The local rag
advises vigilance, supervised child's play.

                    A yellow polka-dot umbrella
                    (Has Number 12's transvestite
                    braved the day?) is the only
                    visible, moving thing.

We keep to the house,
have time on our hands.
The mountains dip into
weather from elsewhere.

                    A Yu-Gi-Oh duel in the bedroom
                    has *Blue-Eyes White Dragon*
                    challenge *Soul of Purity and Light*.

Für Elise chases itself
like the dog stoned by boys
on the transformer roof.

                    We don't know where we are,
                    though twice lately, we used the phrase
                    'a life thought better of'

like flat-packed shelves
that had to be returned
on account of too many bolts,
too much daylight.

The rain claims the green.
Dusk skips over its muck
and blackened trees.

Upstairs, Des takes back *Dark Magician*,
decides he will play *Swordstalker* instead.

Why I Am Not A Nature Poet

has to do with Max and Nemo
scarcely out of a plastic bag three weeks ago
and into our new fishbowl
when Nemo started swelling up,
spiking pineapple fins and lying sideways
like a drunk in a gutter
lipping some foul-mouthed shanty to the moon.
'Dropsy,' Ed in the Pet Centre said, who,
three weeks ago, swore they could live fifteen years.
'Put him in the freezer. Kill him quick.
Don't leave him in the bowl to rot
or the other one will eat him and die too.'
I buy drops instead that cost
what three new goldfish would.
Eve makes a *Get Well Nemo* card
and talks to him when she passes,
calling him 'little guy' and 'goldilocks',
playing 'Für Nemo' on her keyboard.
I don't know. Max, I think, fine-tunes
his hunger and has a bloodless, sly look
to him now. He knows I'm on to him.
I tap the glass, shoo him away
whenever I see him closing in
on Nemo's wide-eyed slump
but I can't stand sentinel all night.
I'm in the kitchen when I hear the shout,
'Come up, see what's going on.'
I take the stairs two at a time,
ordering the right words in my head:
Choice . . . Fault . . . Nature . . . Destiny.
Eve's face is level with the fish
and behind the bowl so it's magnified,
amazed, like an open moon.
'Max is nudging Nemo,' she says.
'He's helping him turn round.'

Theme Park

1 MAY

I just got
a summer job
in a blues band
playing sax
for the wedding waltz
of the skeletal bride
in her narrowing dress
and ashen veil
rocking and pleating
her plain fingers
in perfect time,
growing more wasted
by the hour.

2 JUNE

We live between
the stockpiled passion
of our work routine
and time offstage
when street-sweepers
and engineers
restore to us
thin strategies,
vain dreams.
Between shifts,
she flirts with the
groom's father,
as if tomorrow
will not see her
throw him — and

his stilted son —
off the fiercest
inclines of
her grief.

3 JULY

She has taken to
giving us the slip.
I follow her
to the Saloon,
watch her plot
with old bottles
and a broken can,
cajoling the barman
into one more,
on the tab.
But she's always
back on her throne
by first admission,
just as the erstwhile
father-in-law
bears down
again on his
son's no-show,
our trouble,
the expense.

4 AUGUST

She's gone. All hell
has broken loose.

Will (the Cast Member
with the wayward eye)
found her fallen
wedding dress
this morning.
It's very quiet
without her.
I hear my
false notes
runged like
ladders that
don't take me
anywhere.

5 SEPTEMBER

She isn't missed.
Not even Pop
seems overly upset
though she's
out there now,
seeking the hide
of his doomed,
enchanted son.
For this last week
the lights are down,
we can play what
we please. I fancy
something skittish.
Nothing with
a chink in it:
no waltzes, no
love songs.

Transatlantic

You think one call
from a kiosk
on Clonskeagh Road
will be enough
to cut you loose,
but seventeen years
could pass like geese
over your roof
and you'd wake at five,
your tongue jammed
in the one lie,
the hairs on your
hand straining
towards the line
you held over
thousands of sea-miles
and broke up
over an awkward
dawn that is
rounding
on you
and your
swansong
even now.

Juniper Street

We go to sleep by artificial moonlight.
The floodlit stadium times itself out at midnight
and a thicker weave of darkness plies the room.

We sleep under the eaves, where nights of late
have eddied in the wind's plump, elevated arch.
We wake to only dawn's blindsided glaze.

Just last week, the icicle tree at our door
was in full bloom. The breeze made a show of it.
We picked one bud with the longest stem

to set in the freezer where it has since drooped,
given itself up to the kitchen's heated breath.
Now March is opening and closing, like a valve.

Snow-melt in the gutters keeps new time,
ice slurs on the lean-to, the Swiss Alps
of the swimming pool drape over our own roof line

and the ticking flagpole sees out the month with us.
This morning, the trash was dappled on the lawn
where squirrels are sifting with Victorian aplomb,

tails aloft like pinkies off a cup. Chrome riplets from
next door's chimes, like first notes of some oriole
or wren, slip over the path, are pounced on by a hawk

in the gingko preening himself to call upon a light
just come into its own. Then the laburnum school bus
swerves into view, and the children's on-the-run

goodbyes settle on the porch with my unplanted kiss.
I am queen of the morning: nothing to do but to fiddle
words or quote the gilt-edge of our neighbour's forsythia

gaining on our own trim laurel shrub. Or tell you now
that even in January, with our snow-boots lined up
in the hall, I slipped your leather glove onto my hand

and felt the heat of you as something on the turn
that would carry us over the tip of all that darkness
and land us on the stoop of this whole new world.

Glaze

A frozen river after a night of rain:
   a skim of ice no bigger than your breath
has a single bird on it that is stalled,
   sleek as my breastbone, indelibly alone.
Do you know it yet, who rustled songbirds
   out of winter and once sparked a hummingbird?
What now of the cold on your wingtip,
   the ice on your tongue? With your eye setting
on where I still you, I all but turn away.

The Annotated House

The window is flush with words, but my page
hangs limp as the snow cloud slouching over
Carlo's house. I am killing time between lines
I have written in dust on the sill. Sometime
before evening, I will shift in this chair, shake out
my stockinged feet, put down my book and ask
the porch screen something pointed but oblique.

Or else, I will take myself off to lie in a bed
silken with usage, beneath a cover laced
with verbs for getting on. In truth, there is
nowhere to go from here. The treads and risers
of every line return me to a carpet scheming
with print. One wrong foot, and there's
no telling what months heaped in the basement —
like laundry thinned by colour — will reveal.

A sequence of breath cuts a dash in the hall.
In the kitchen, the evening bucks its rhythm
and lull. Even the grammar of branches
can't be pinned down. As the smoke flirts
with meaning and falls back into disarray
above the clean, straight-talking roofs,
so my pen, scratching through loose-leaves,
comes to a dead stop at the very moment when
the boiler downstairs, like breaking news,
shunts the here and now into one full clause.

The Letter 'd'

A thriftstore Olympia
with a flaw: one key,
shy of impact, won't strike true.

We learn the run of it,
a written life that manages without,

that compensates for absence,
prefers the present tense,
forgets itself in coping with just this.

Acknowledgements

To my mentor, Victor Quigley (as always, Vic);
to the staff and management of McAuley Meats;
to St Theresa's (for getting me back to where I am);
to Miles (my personal God); to the Chinese Postal Service;
to my dog Jerome; to the estate of Jennifer P Chaser
(whose *One-Toward Joy* has helped so very much);
to Sally and Jack for feeding me (but Sal, *anchovy quiche?*);
to 'From the Margins' Poetry Competition, for seeing
"haunting strains" in 'Inside Out' (1st Prize 1995),
and, again, in 'Outside In' (3rd Prize 1996);
to the publications that aired some of my poems:
The Dundark Business Guide (2000), *Quagmire Quarterly*,
Rubberneck Review, and the inexhaustible *yourpoemshere.com*.
Almost last (but *never* least): to Belt-Up Books
for their patience and their (still-to-come) slim cheque.
Leaving you, dear reader, who brings us both to this:
you, my friend, I could not begin to thank.

In Passing

Maybe nothing now will pass on the lawn
but another hour, parading its gold chain,
clinking its shadows. Yesterday, it was a boy
in a baseball cap picking something yellow
from the grass. Tomorrow, perhaps a man
and woman, small talk playing into their hands,
ignoring this window, my one taken liberty.
The same tense does for both, literally,
if not for what comes between them:
a darkness planted by me on a whim,
mindful of ink passing through my pen
to spill what's written on what will remain.

Ghosts

What is it this time: milky voices before dawn;
a door hung up on two bars of folksong,
a swingball flicking in between backhands?

I've gambled once too often on an unhinged wind,
on wisps of traffic in the after hours
with their dragged haul of names and messages.

There it is again: the exact blue of a hyacinth
forced out of season. In a shadow crimpling
the indoor step, I have made myself out.

Everything I own would say as much,
even the cypress tree inside the wall
that mutters as I type, 'To me, to me'.

A Dream of Wind

The wind addles my house
as though it were no more than a baby's rattle
and everything I own inside
just plastic beads tossing themselves
in an orange dome that amplifies
and closes down their bright, too-urgent spin.

The wind bends my house
at the knuckle of the stairs
so the top floor wags and straightens
like a palm tree in a hurricane
that has outgrown even the name

of a small boy sleeping, one finger
curled around a plastic arc
jingling in his yellow breath,
the heft of his wren-breast
a litter of notes on a xylophone
blown down from a high shelf.

Re-gifting

Found: in *Title Page — Used and New Books*,
Rosemont, PA, a translation by Vladimir Nabokov
of poems by Pushkin, Tyntchev and Lermentov,
published London, 1947. A snip at twenty bucks.

Given for a 50th, to 'my Boris more-than-Godunov'
from Anna, 'Because of Pushkin, because of love';
then again, in 1986, to 'my dear Joseph
who, tomorrow, will be heading off
to Moscow. From Alex. PS see above'.

Acknowledgements

Acknowledgements are due to the editors of the following publications where these poems, or versions of them, have appeared: *The Bend, Canadian Journal of Irish Studies, The Irish Times, Japanese Journal of Irish Studies, Metre, New Hibernian Review, New Irish Poets* (Bloodaxe, 2004), *New Republic, Poetry Daily, PN Review, Poetry Ireland Review, Poetry London, Poetry Review, Poetry Wales, A Public Space, The Recorder, The Shop, Sunday Miscellany* (RTÉ Radio), *Times Literary Supplement, turnrow* and *Verse*.

Eleven of these poems were published as *Windmill Hymns* by Metre Editions (Metre Magazine, 2004). 'Athlones' was published by Phoenix Poetry Pamphlets in 2004.

'Archaeology' was runner-up in the TLS/Blackwell's Poetry Competition in 2003. 'The Local Accent' was shortlisted in the Best Single Poem category of the Forward Prize, 2004.

The author acknowledges receipt of a grant from An Chomhairle Ealaíon / The Arts Council of Ireland in 2004.

Thanks are due to the staff of the Tyrone Guthrie Centre, Annaghmakerrig, where several of these poems were completed.